MAGNIFLYING GLASS
Coloring Book

A Completely Random Adventure in Coloring Book World

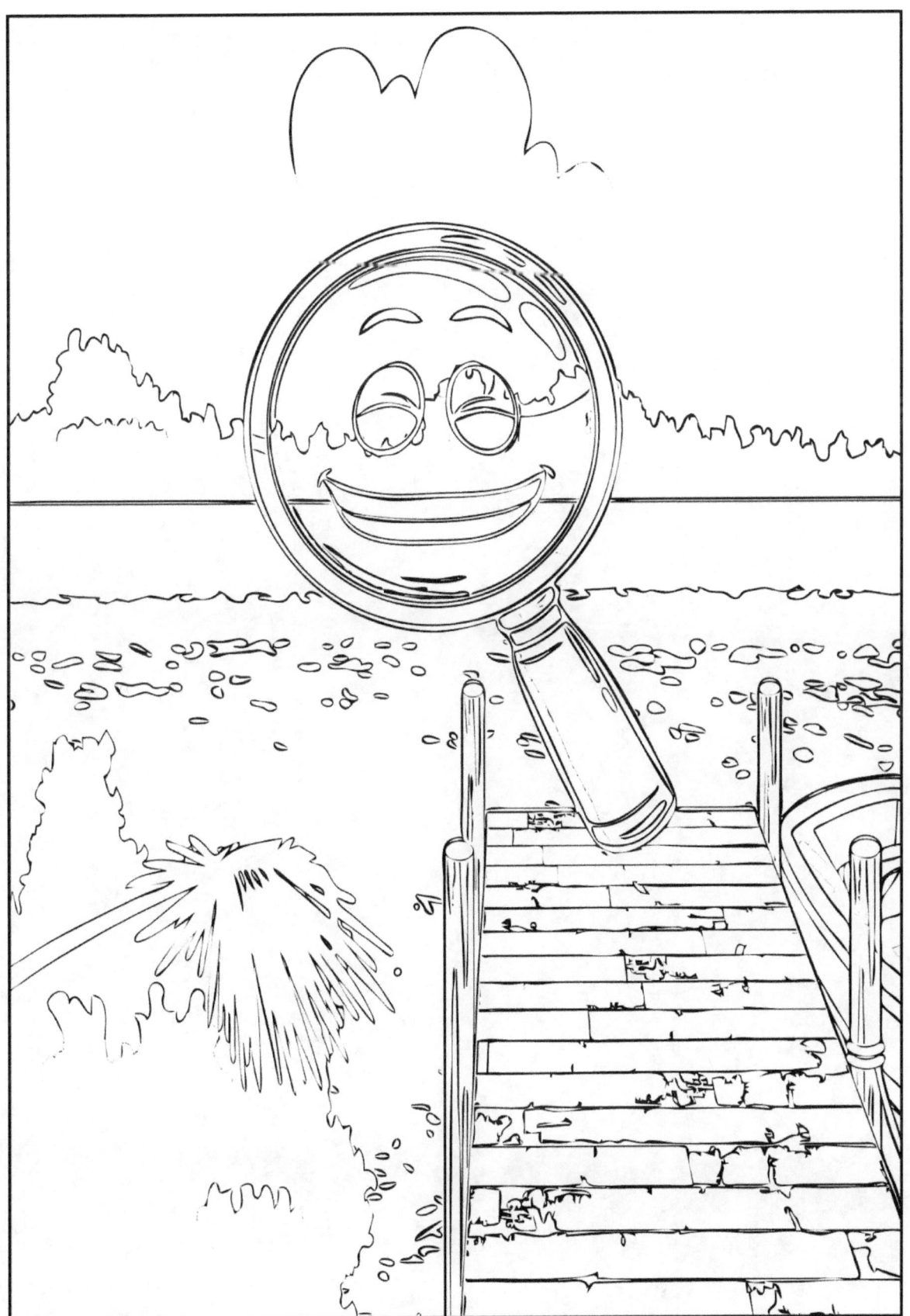

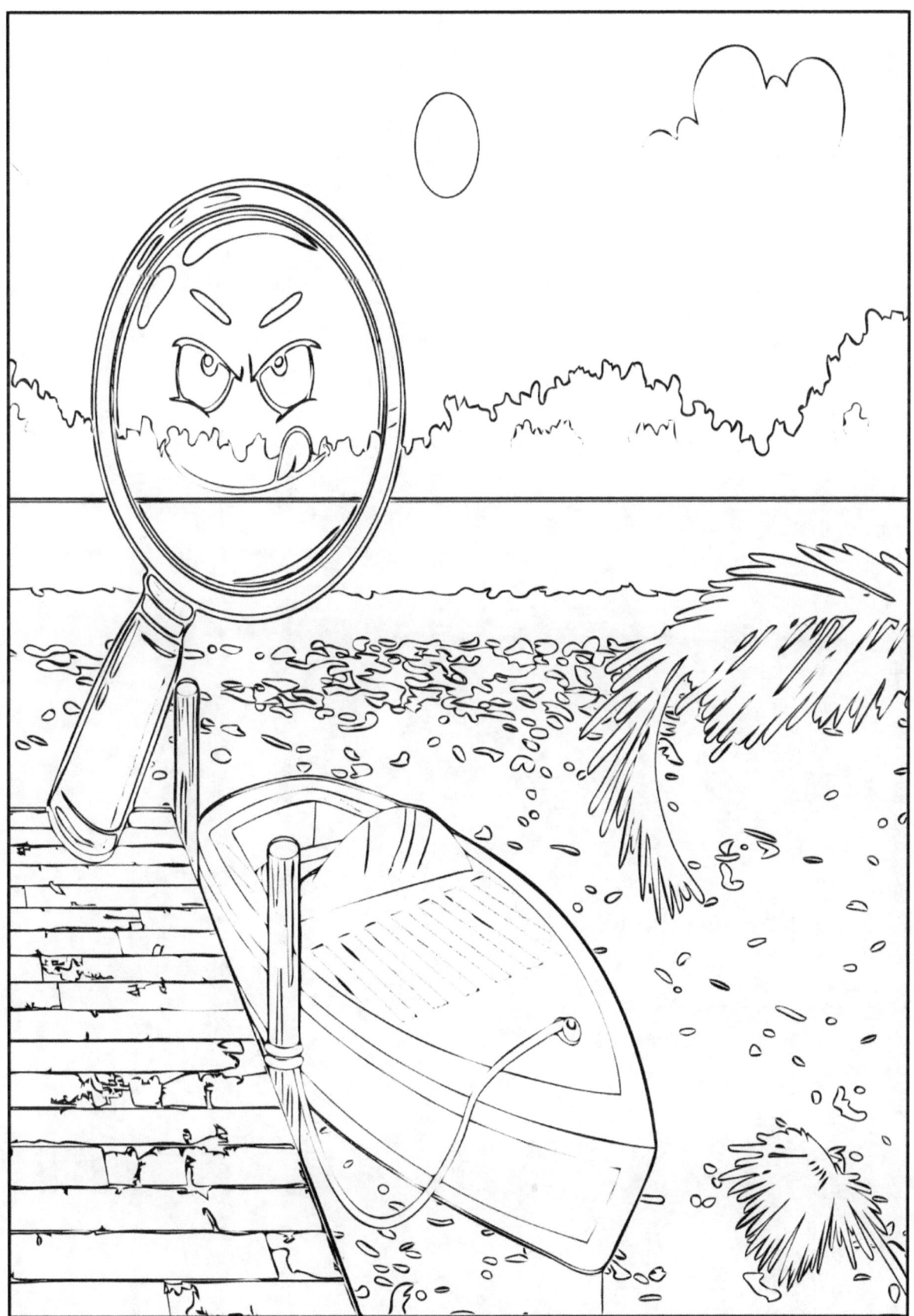

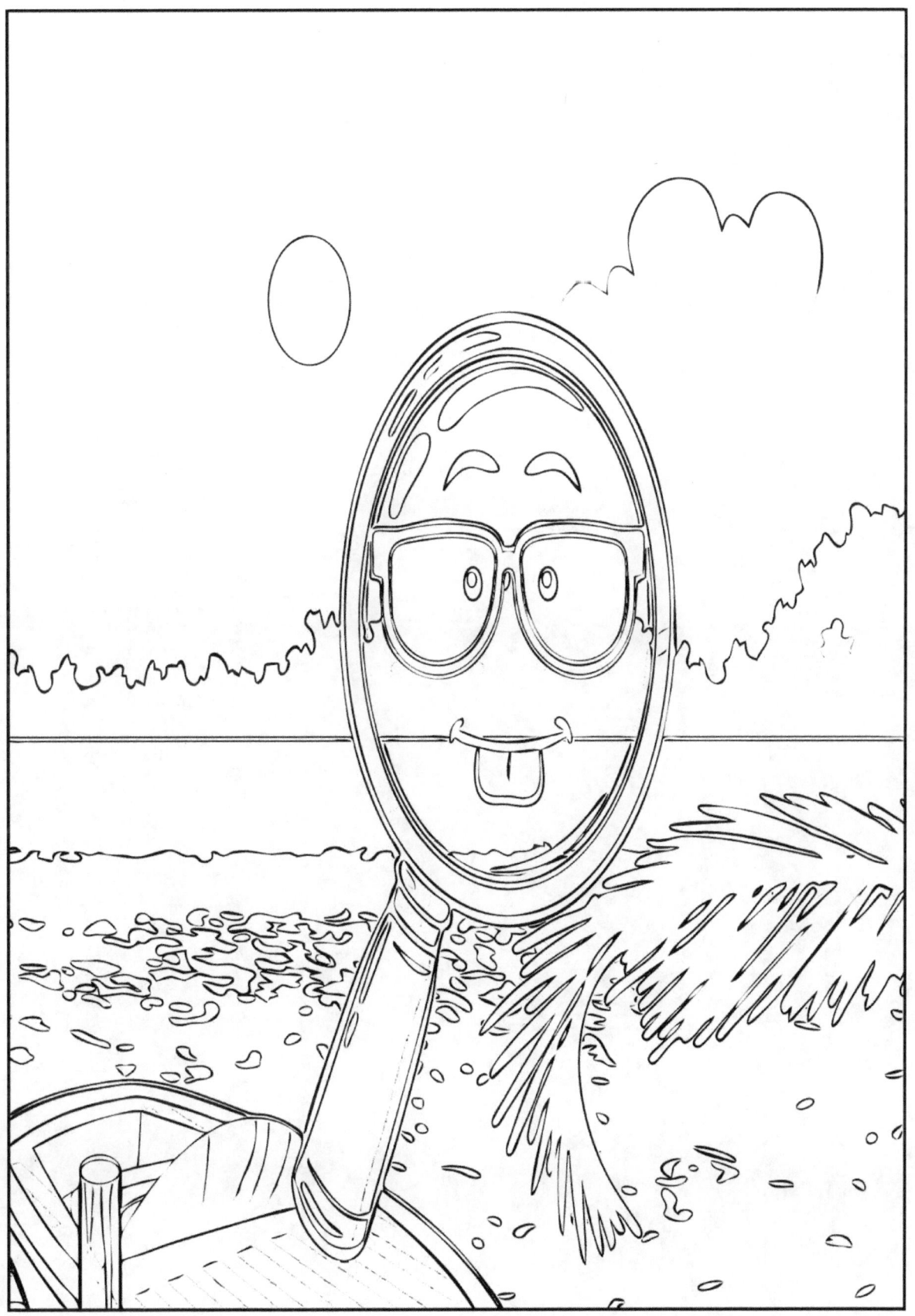

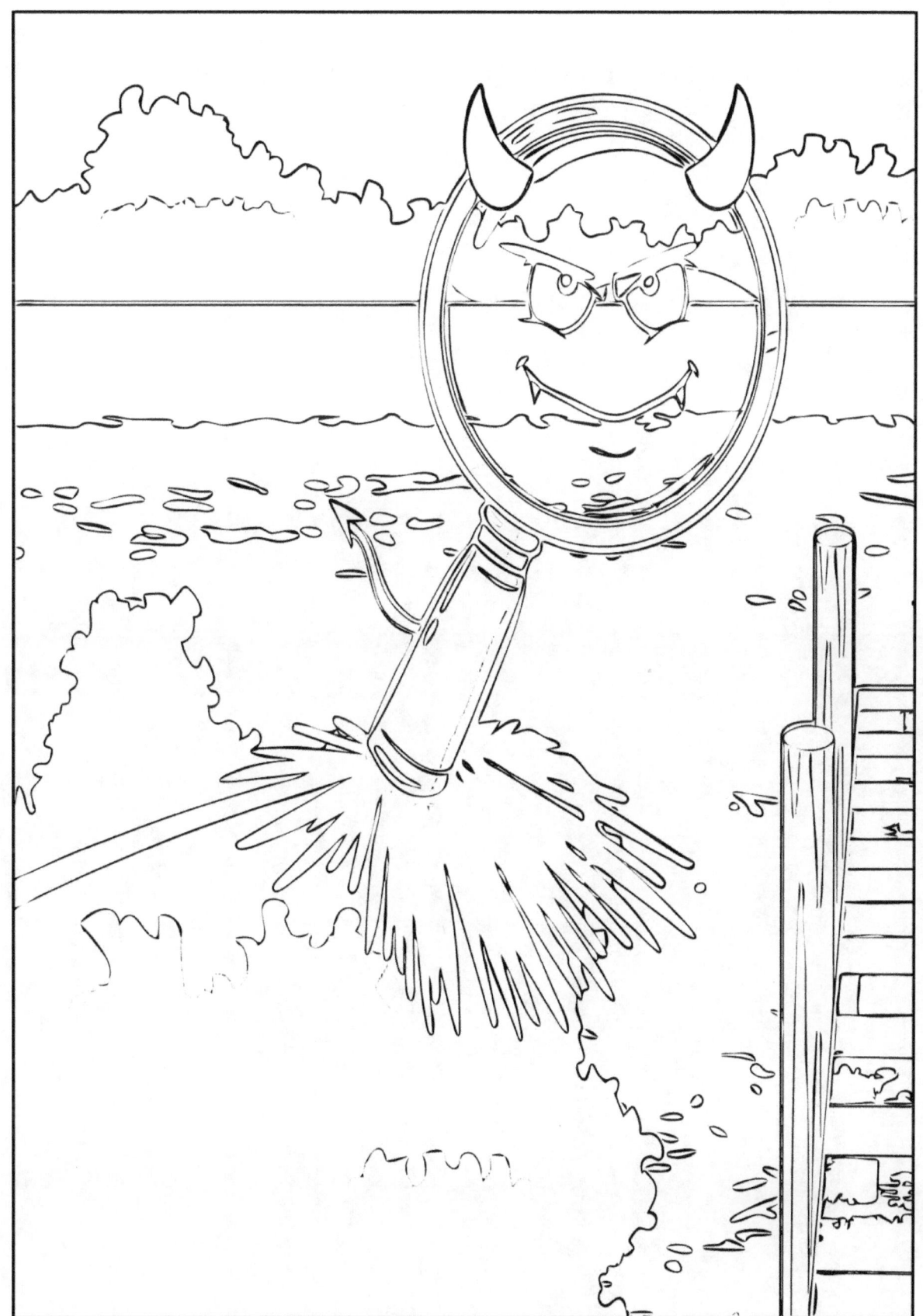

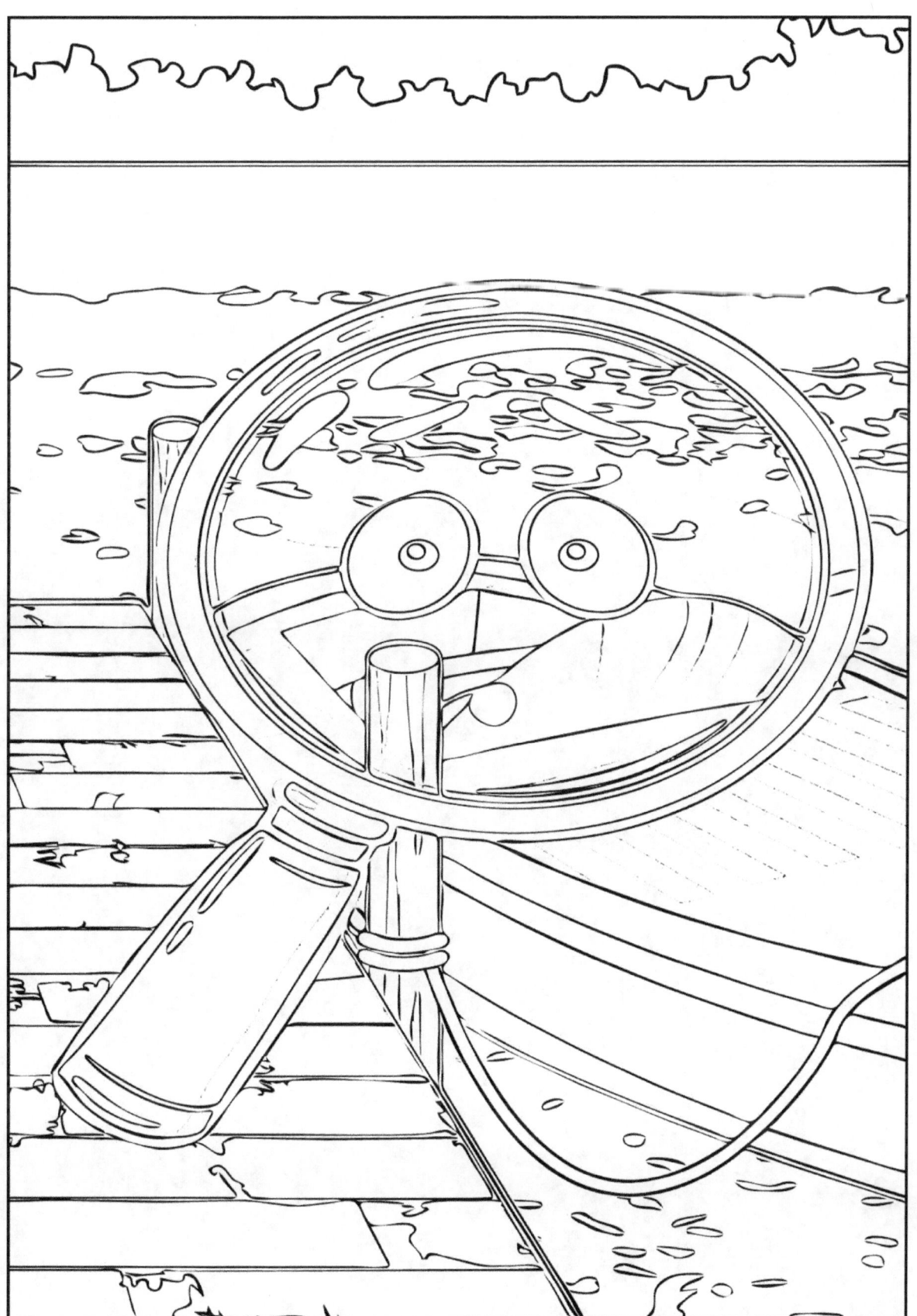

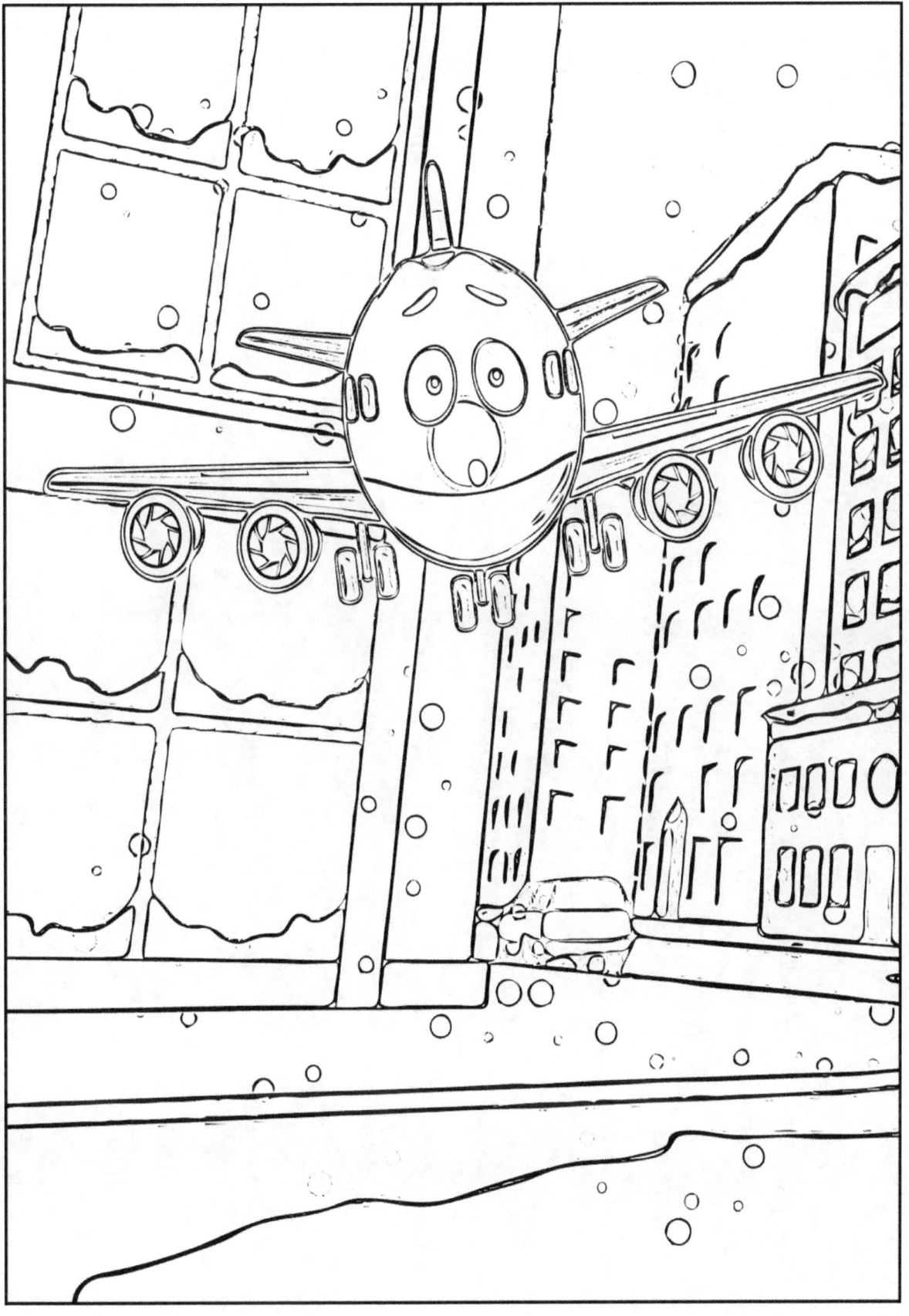

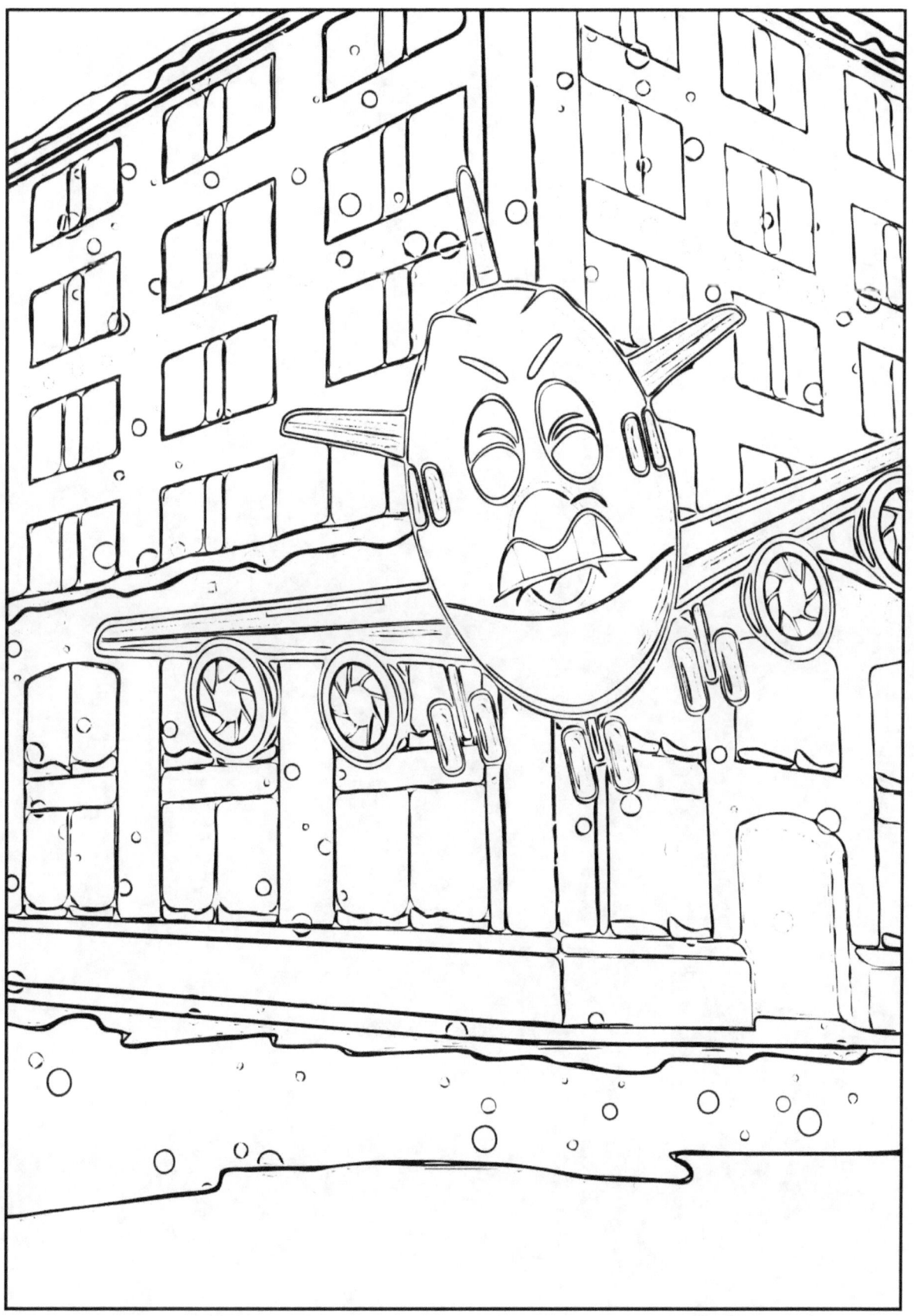

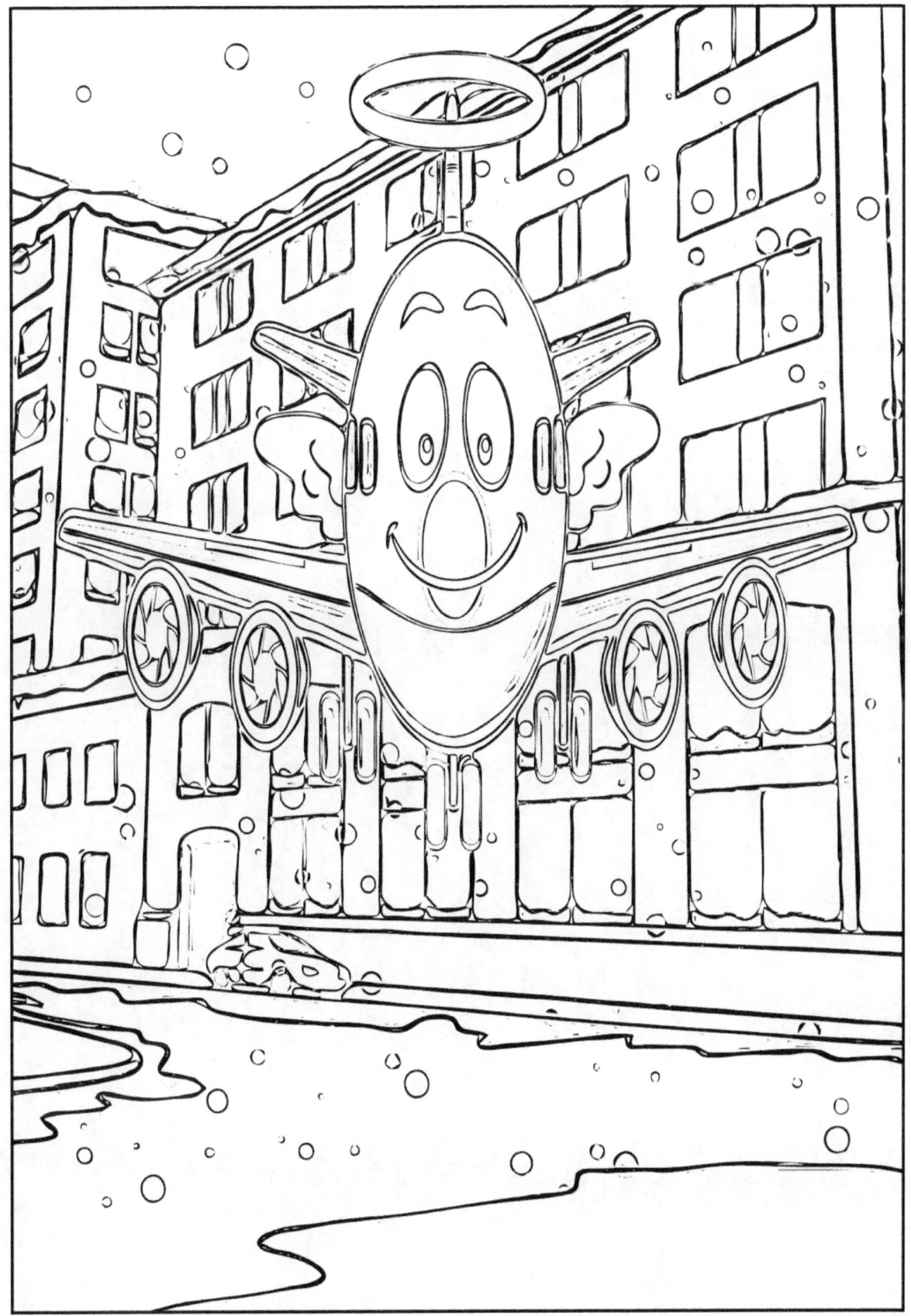

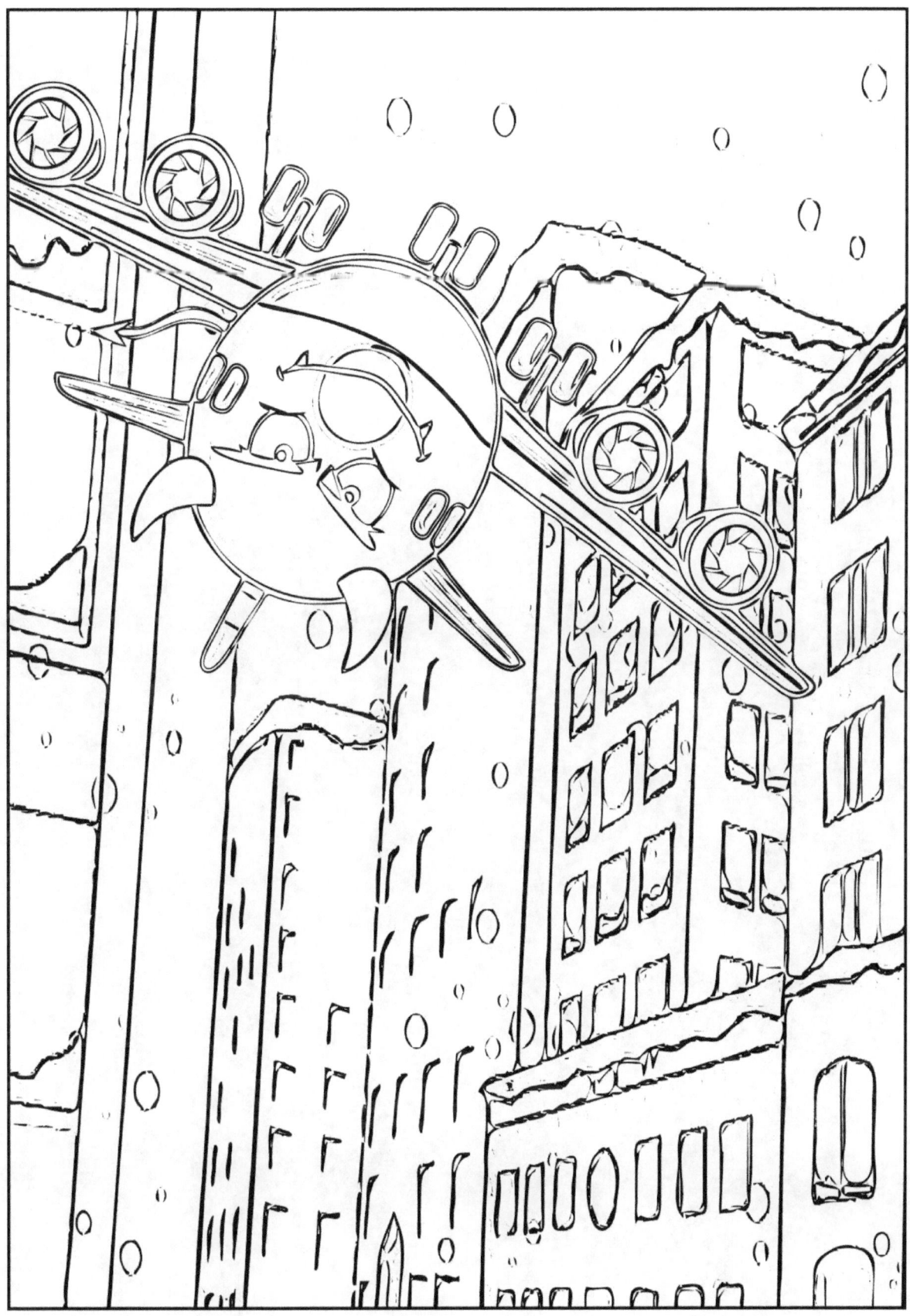

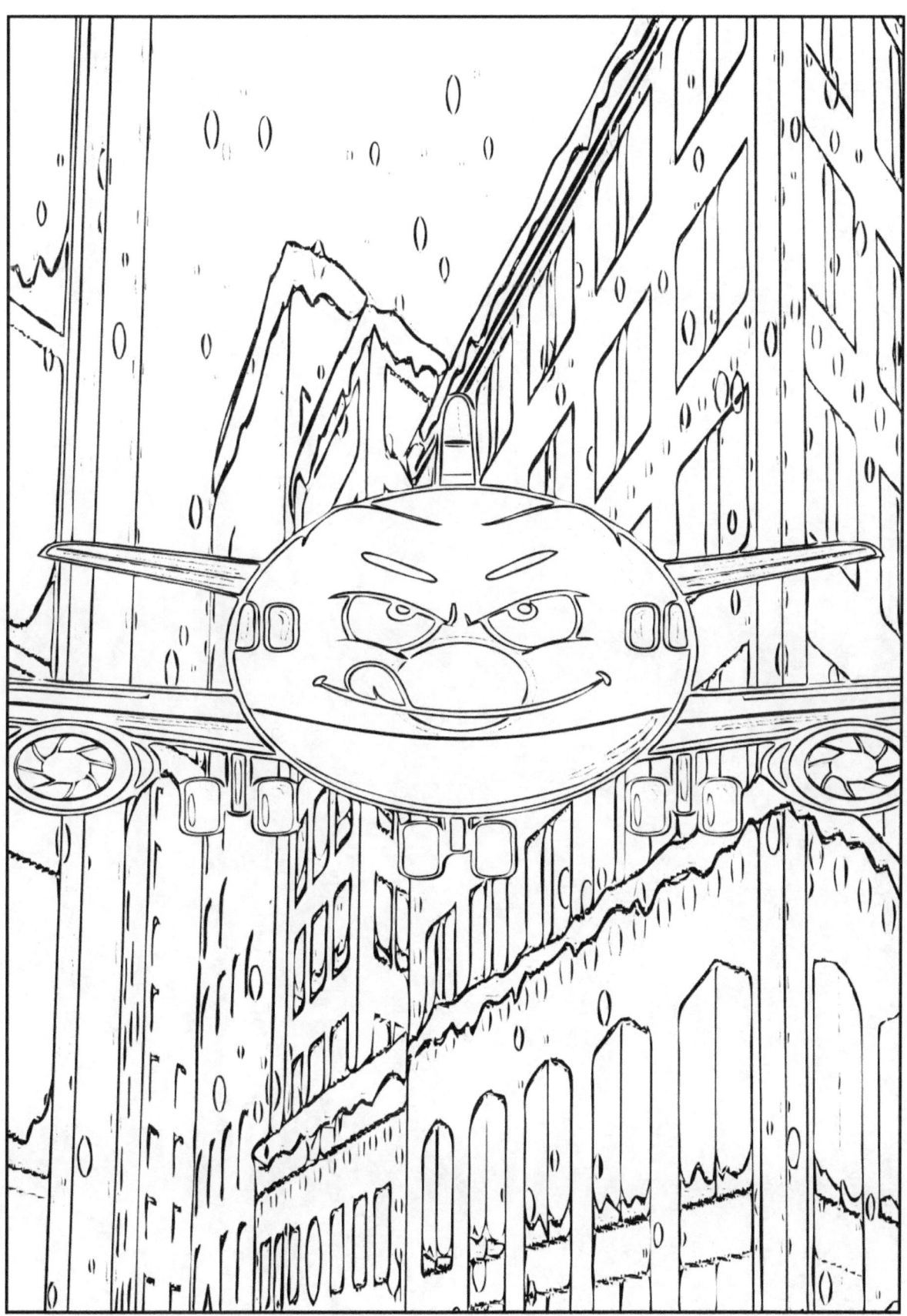

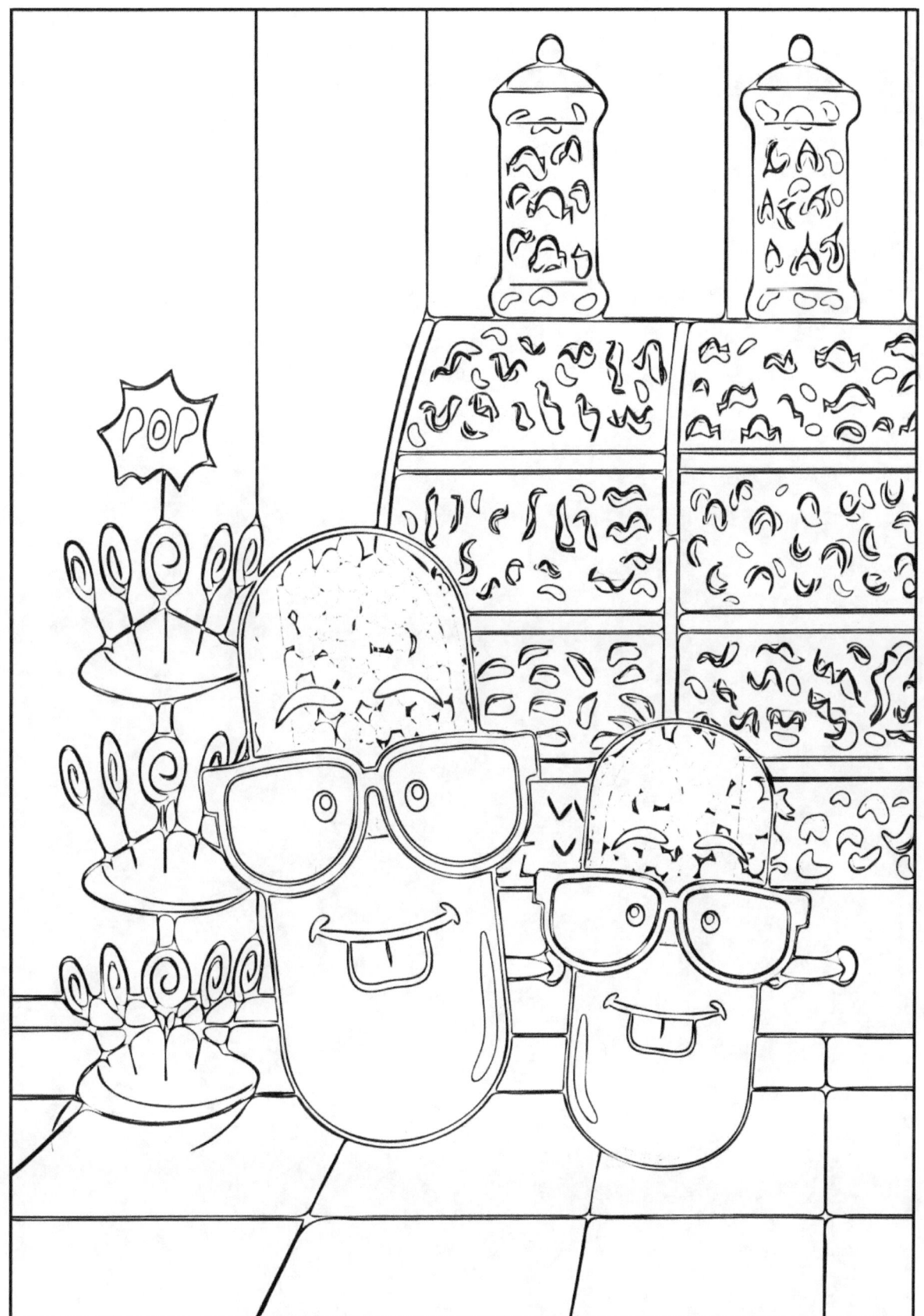

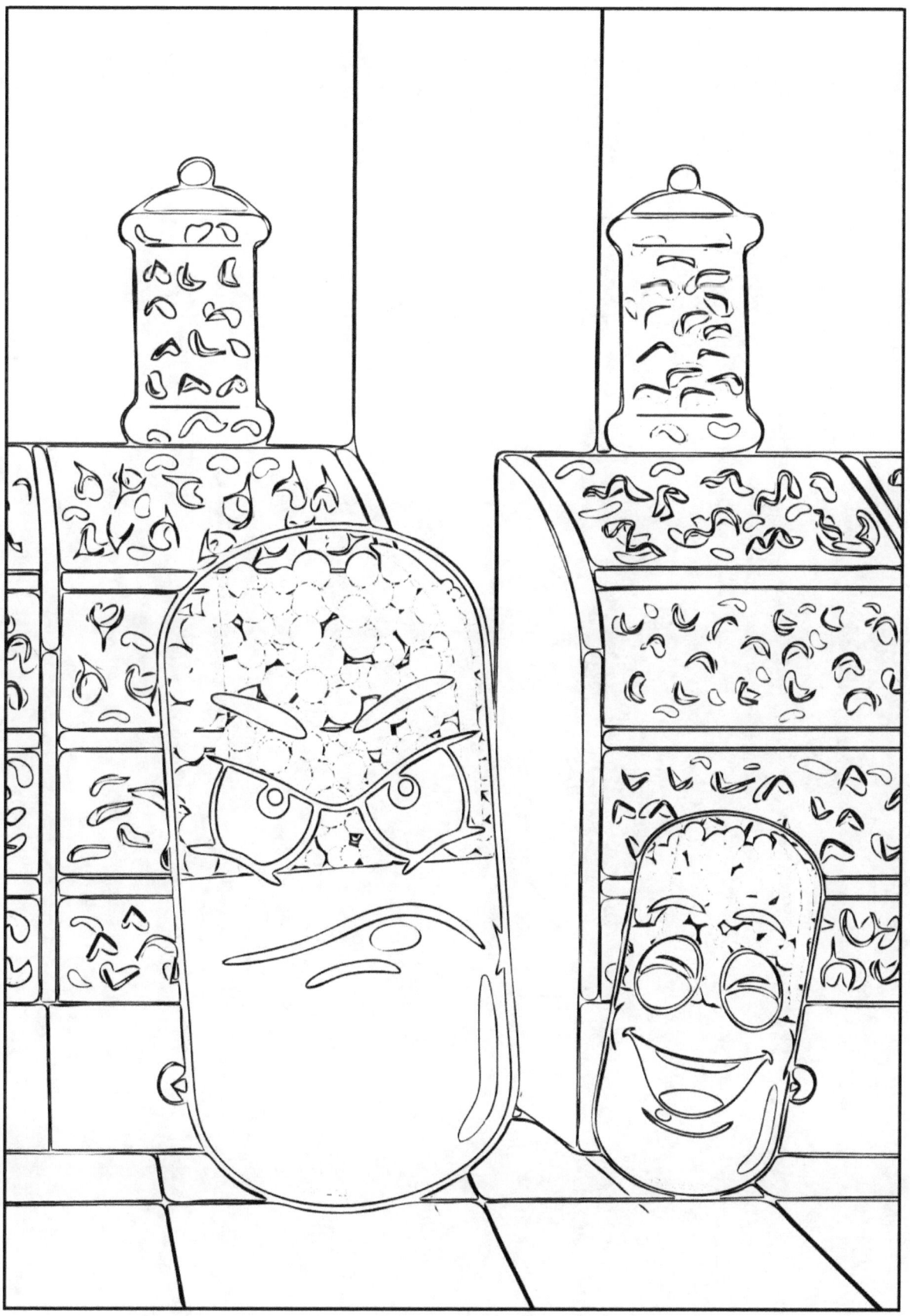

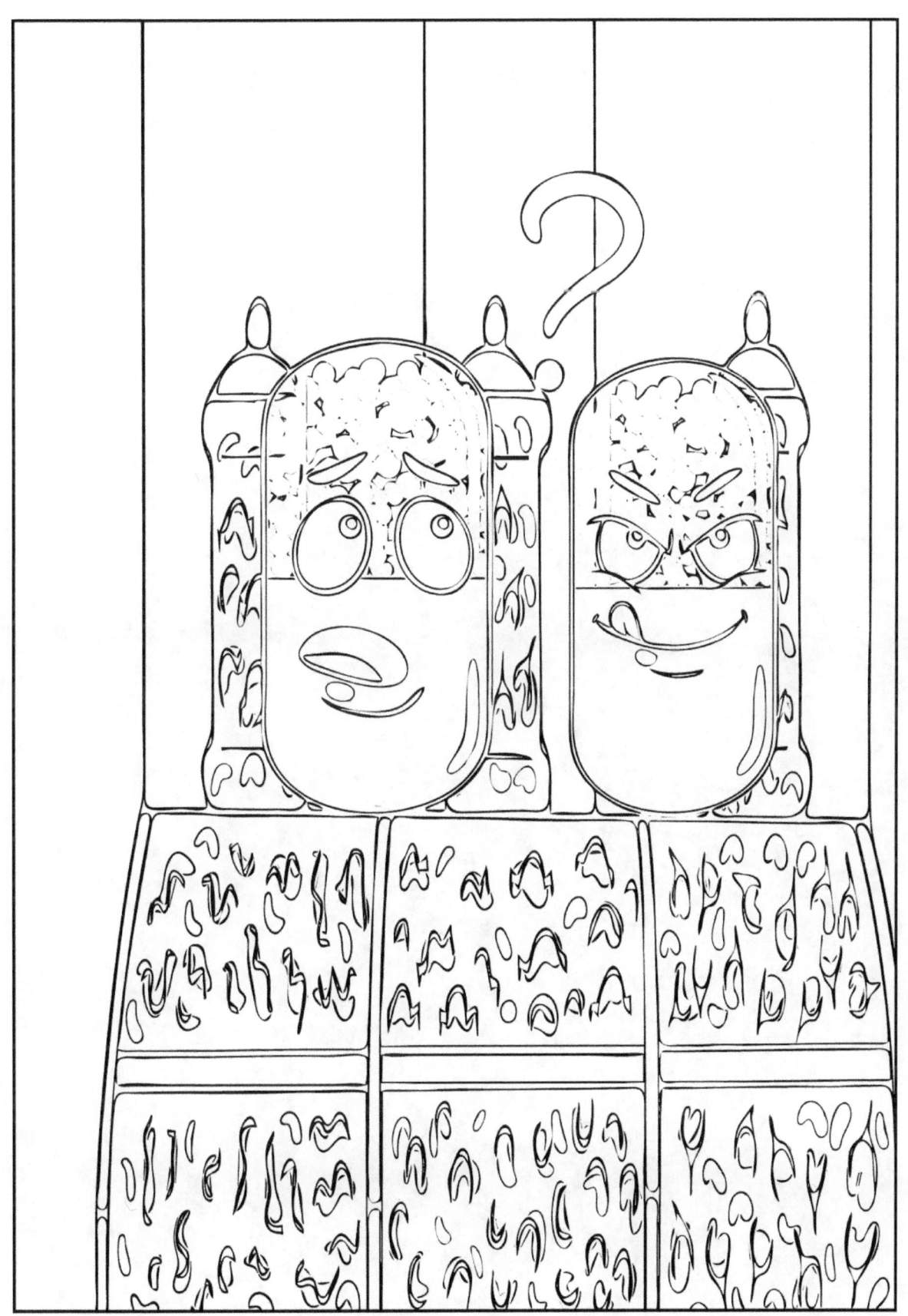

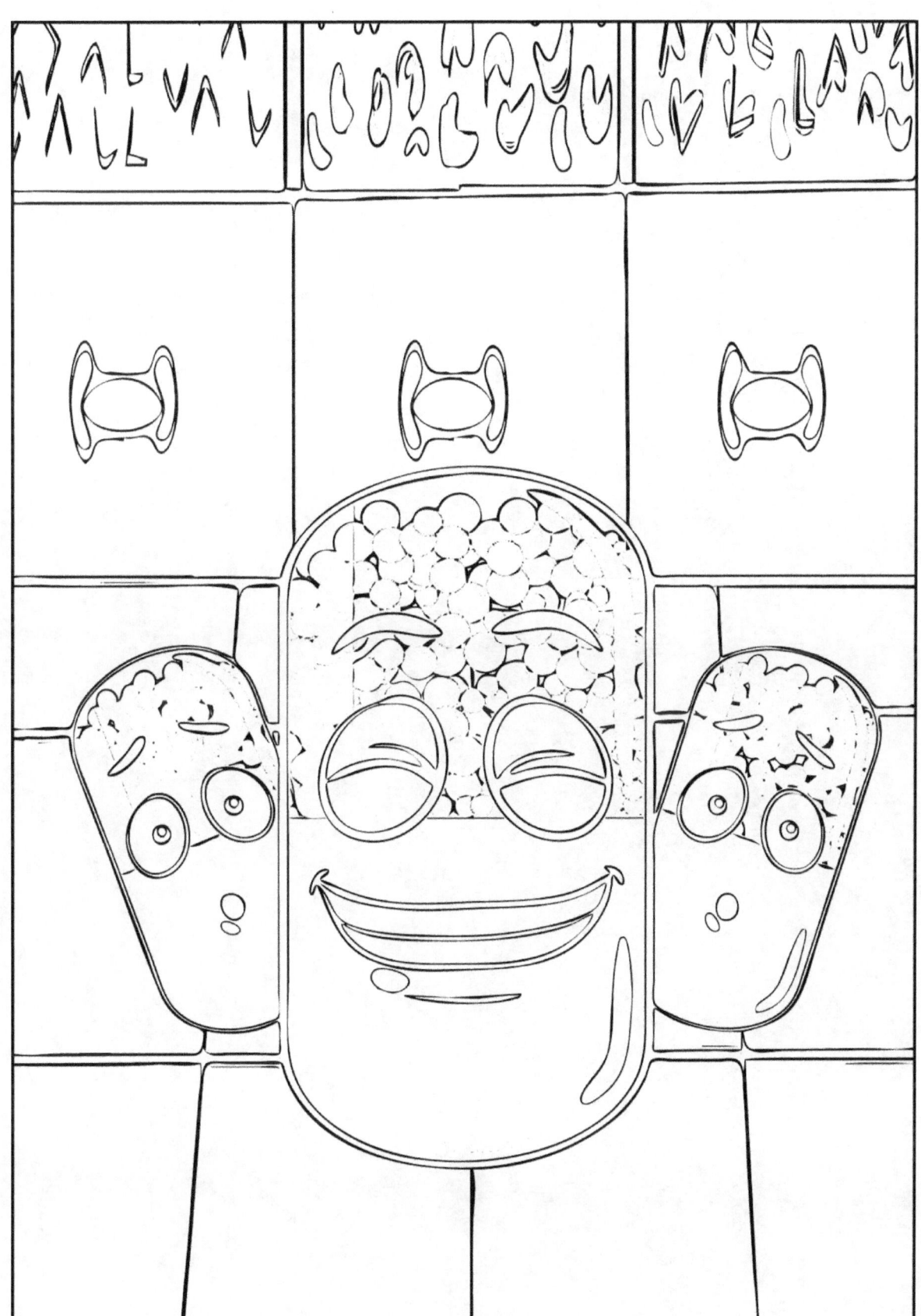

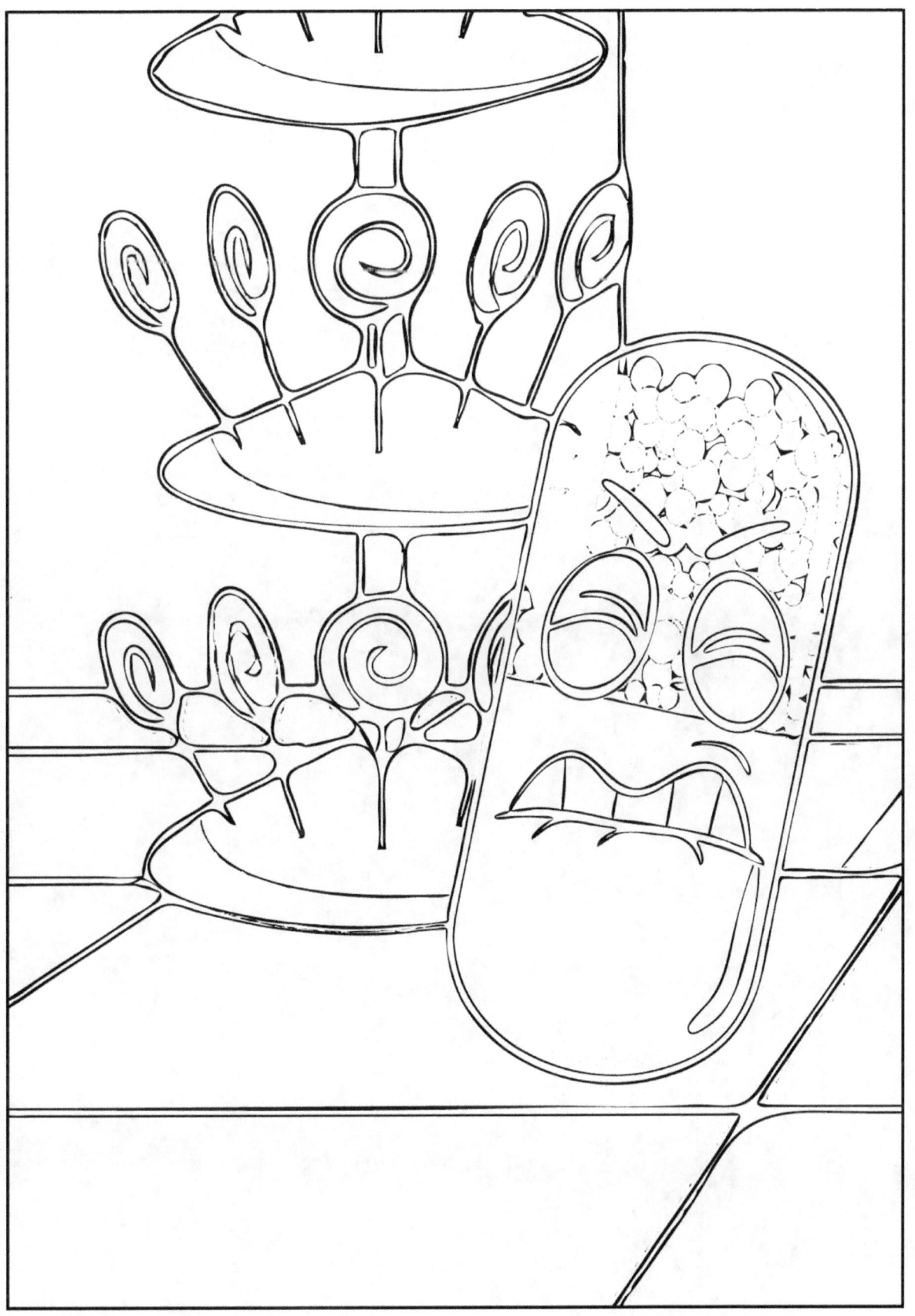

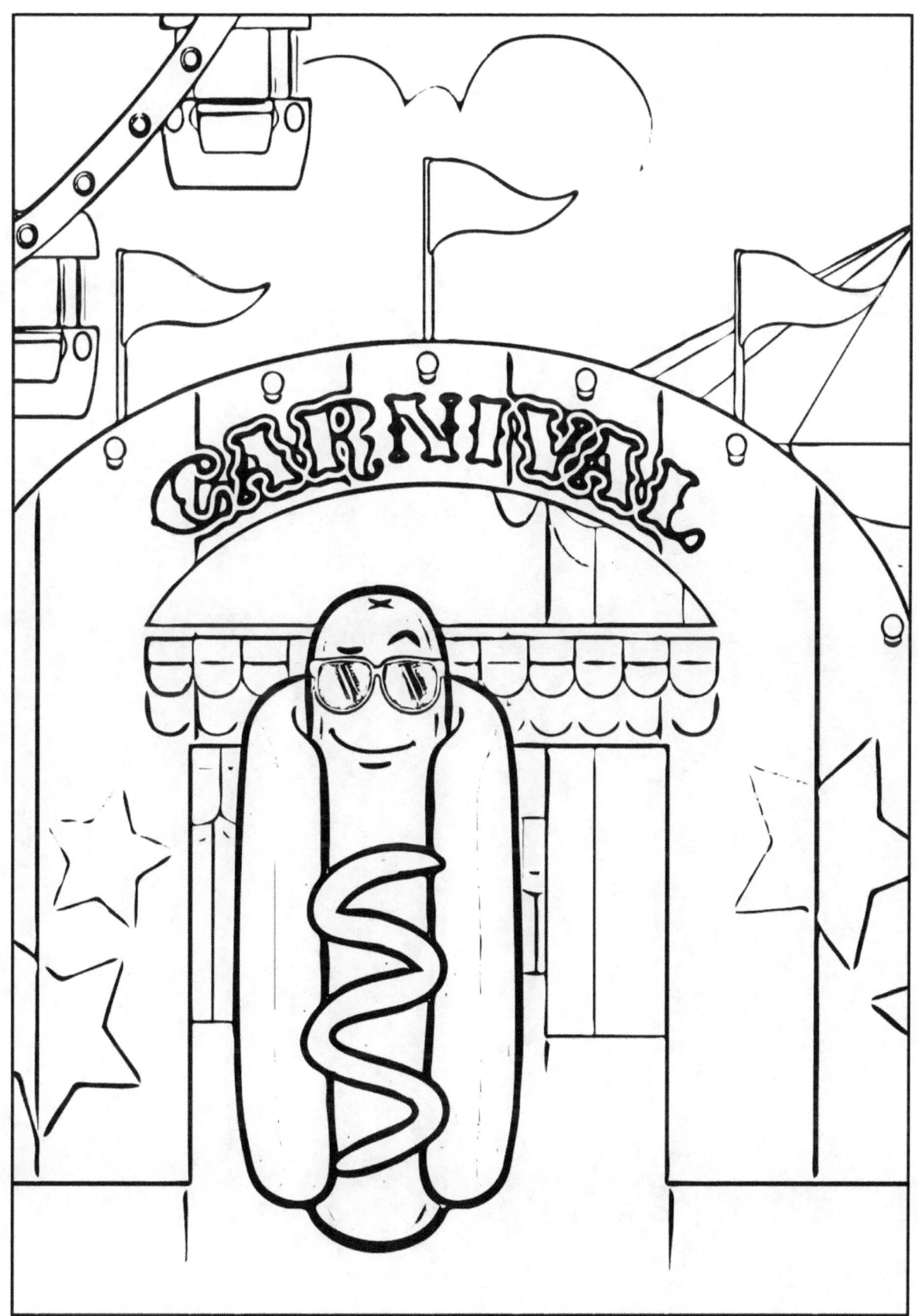

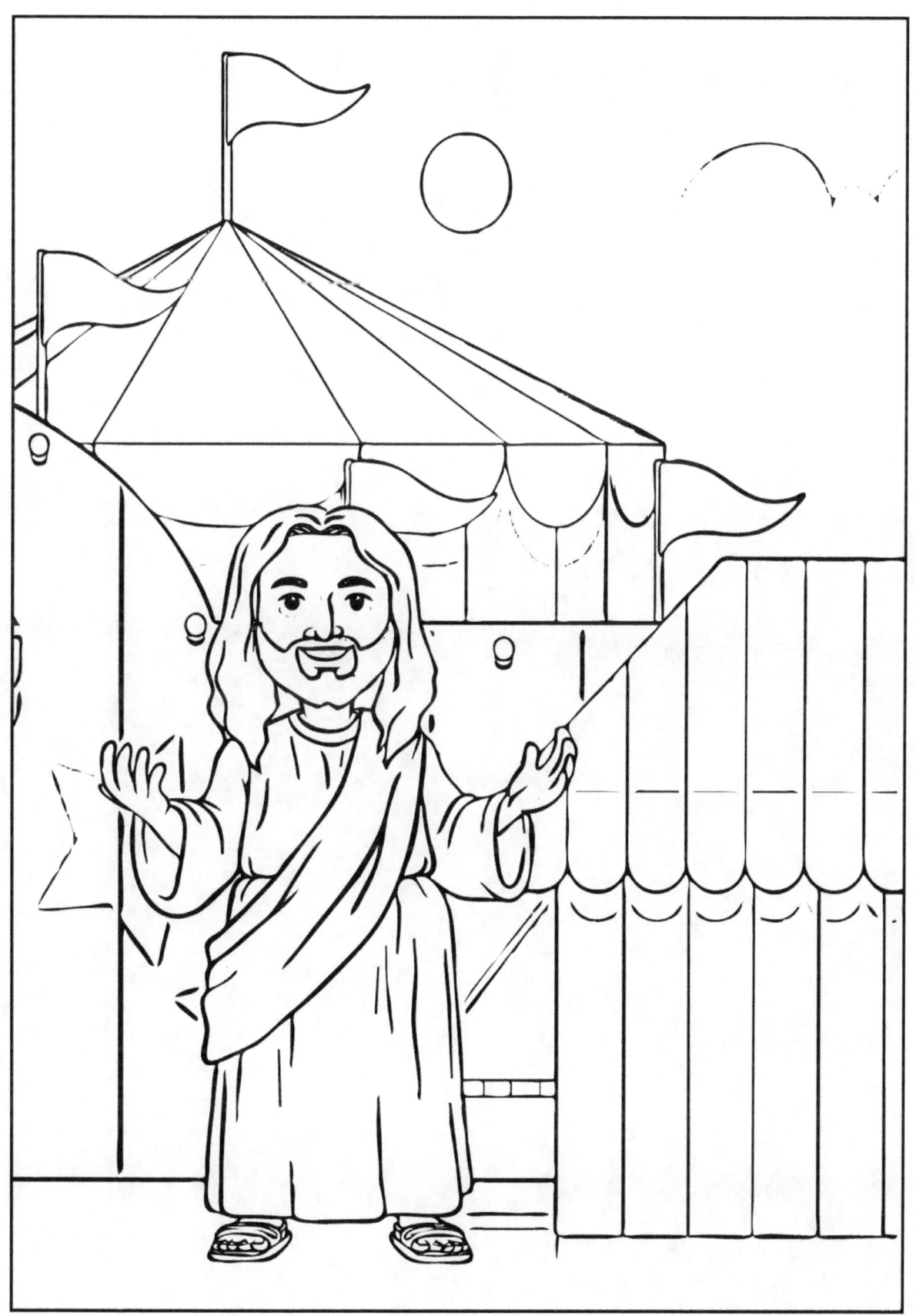

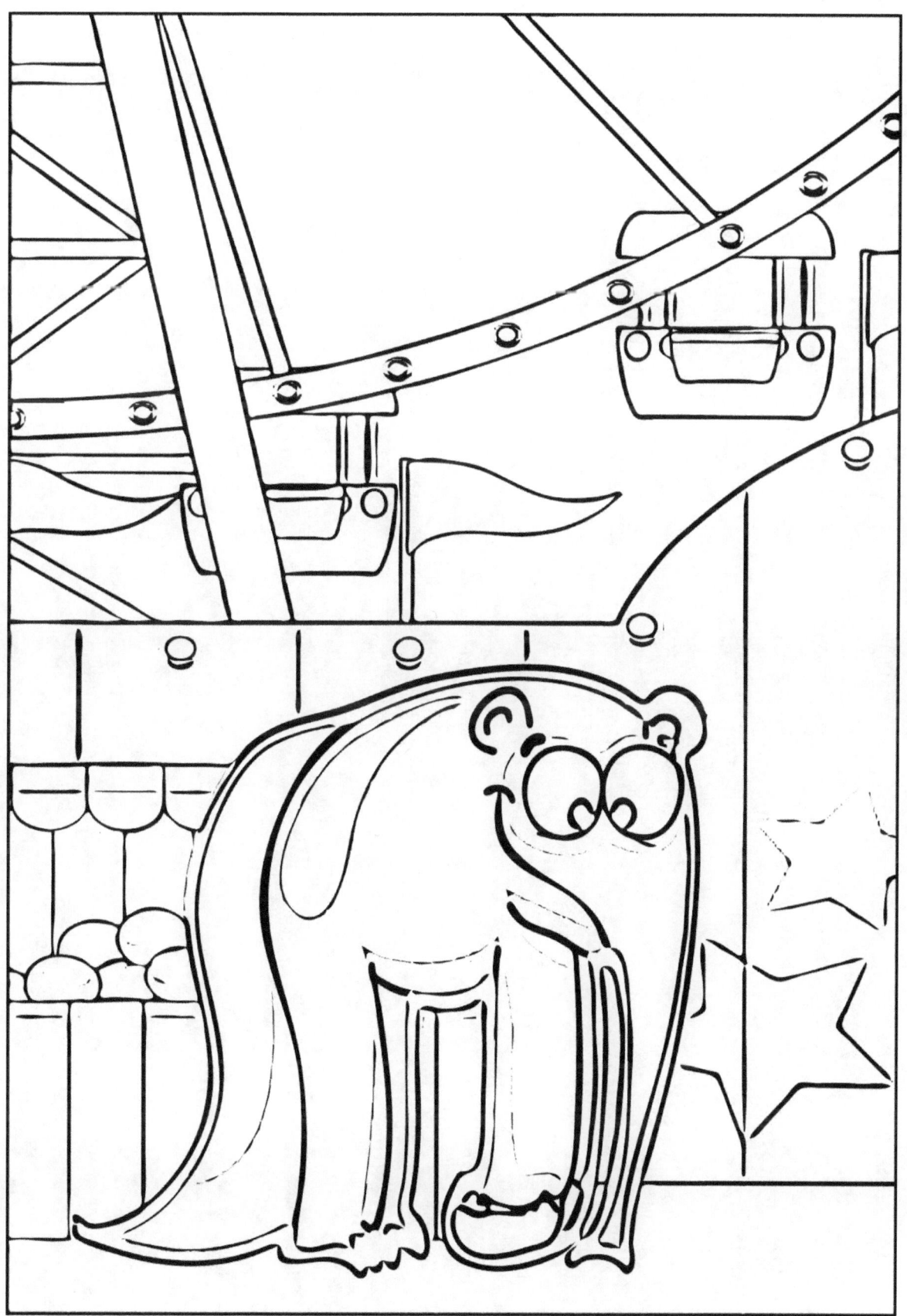

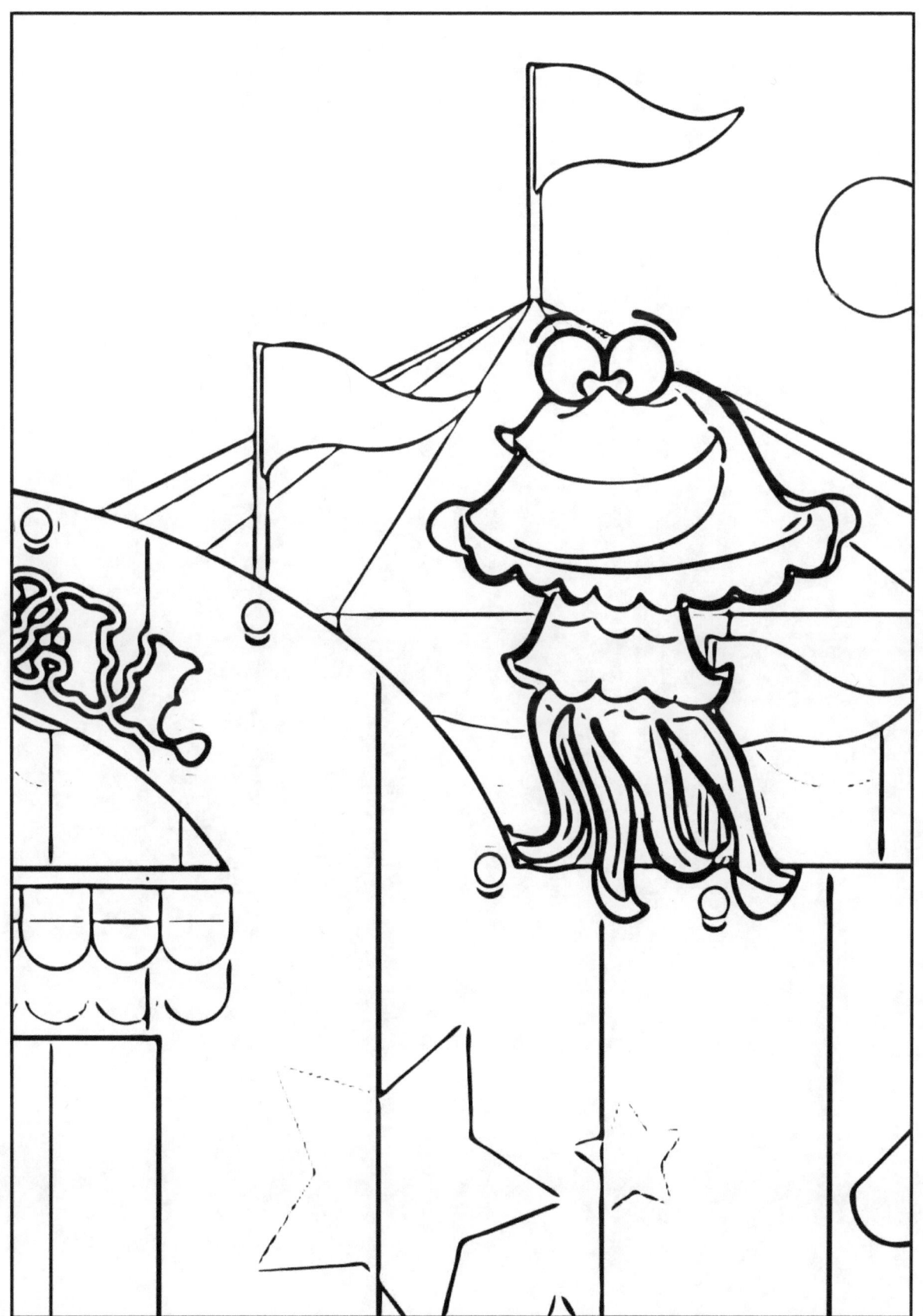

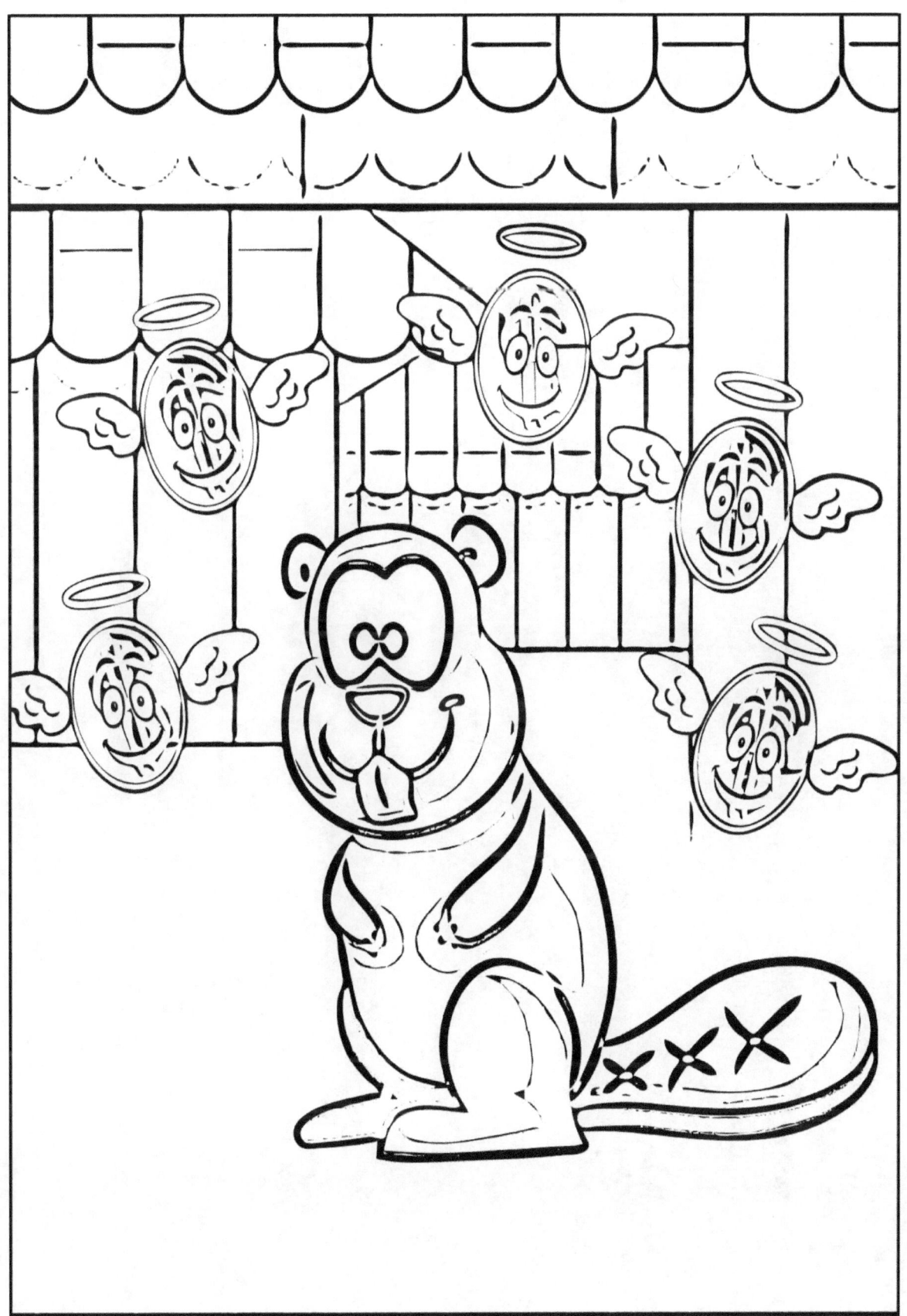

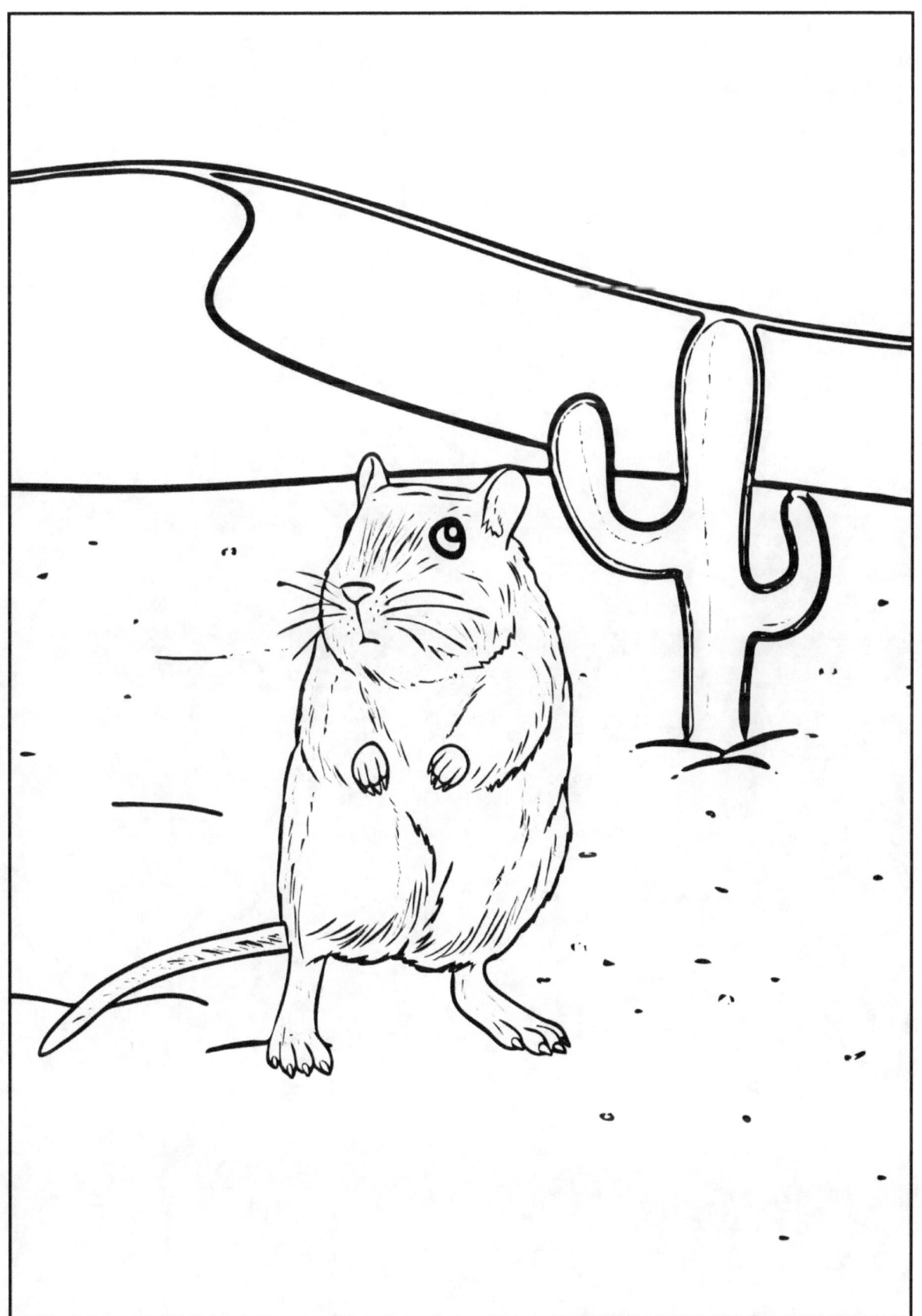

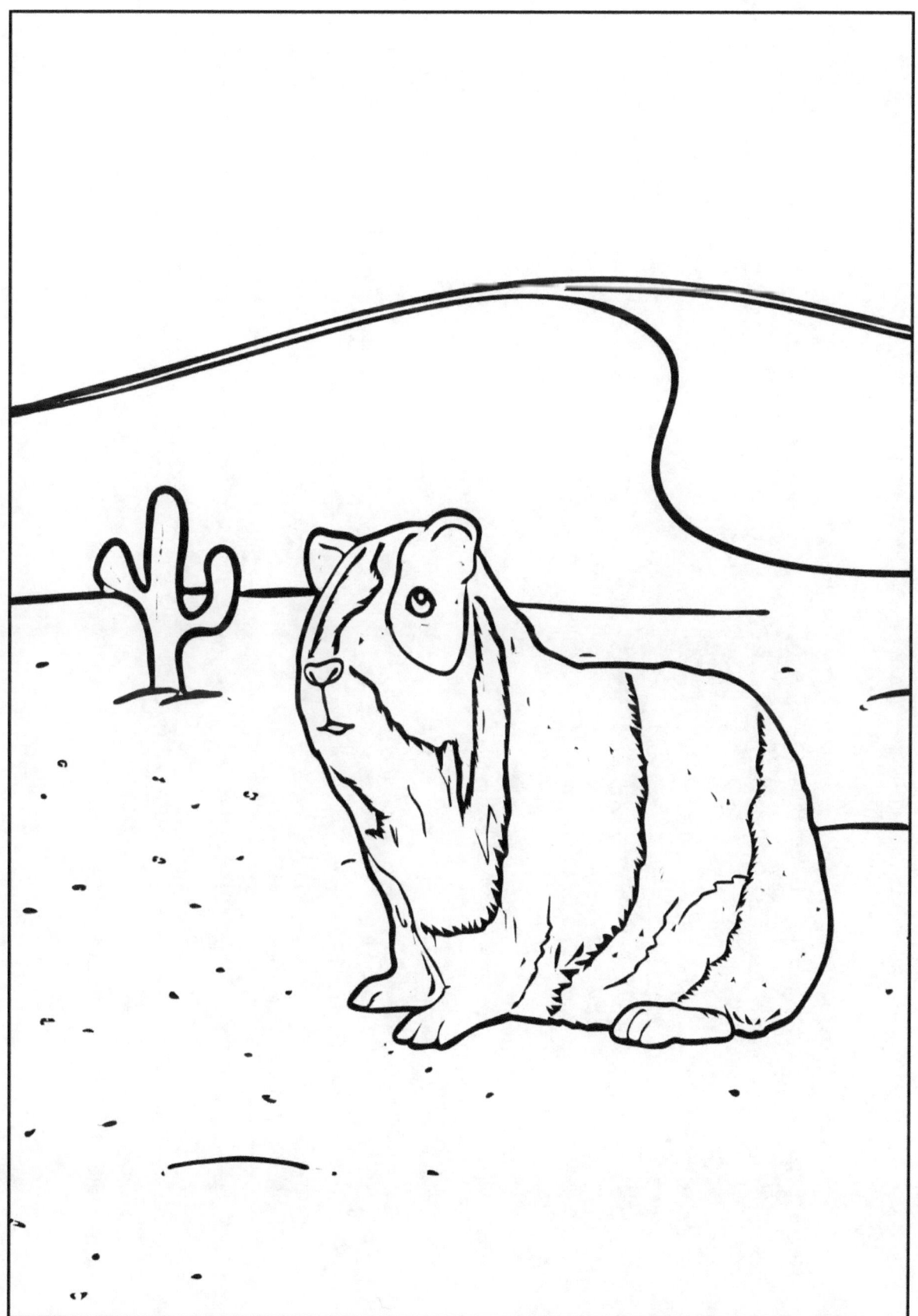

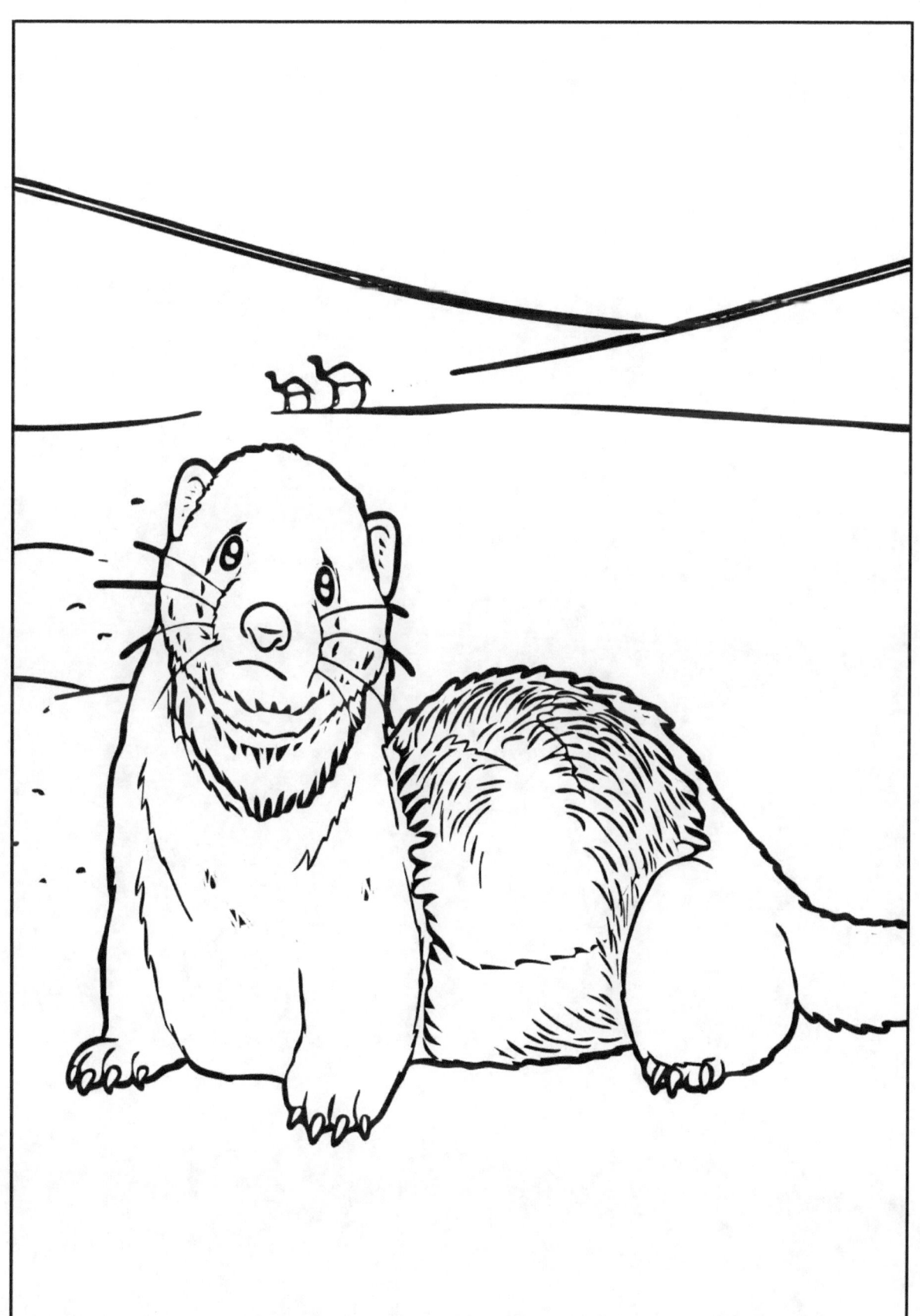

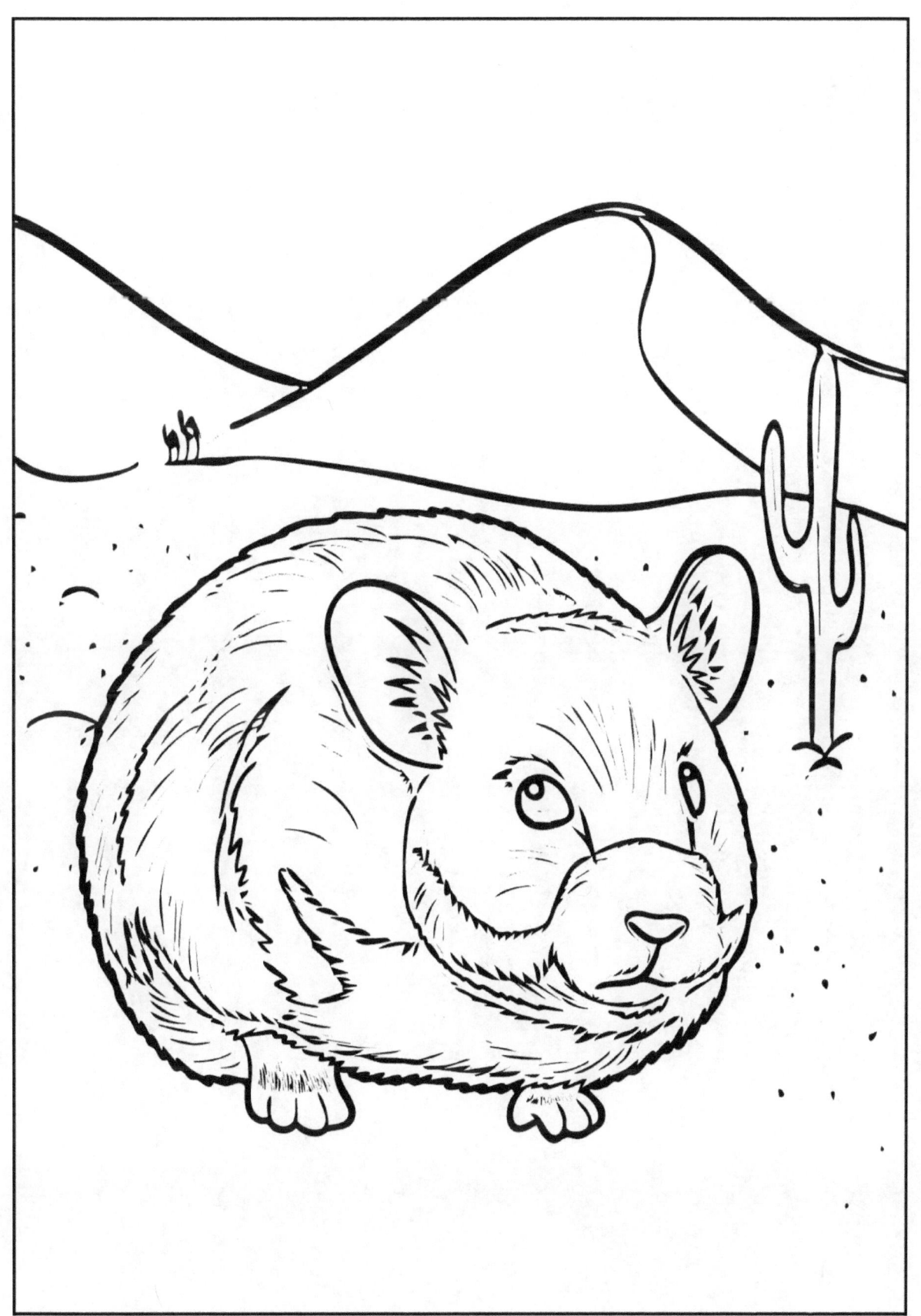

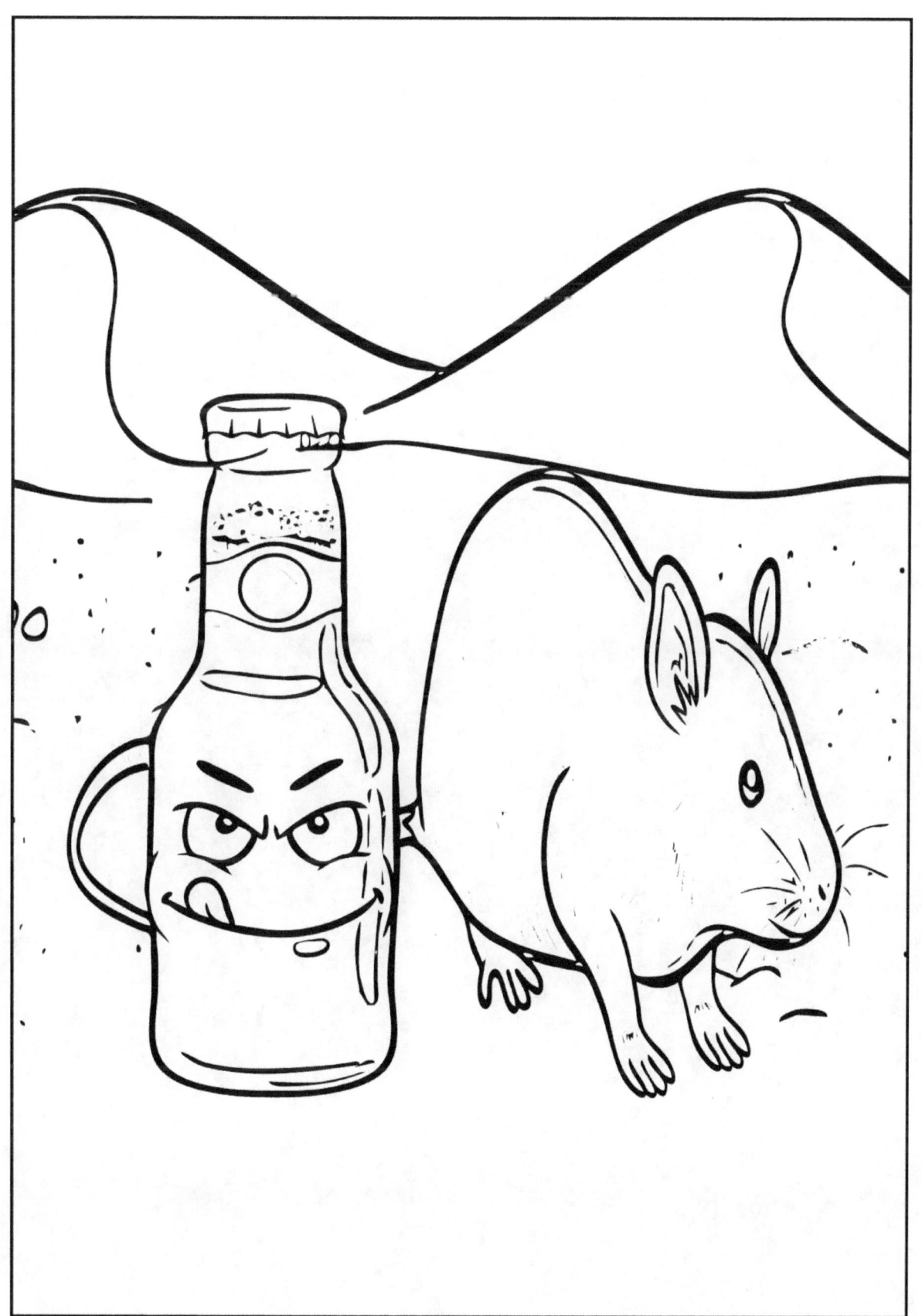

www.ingramcontent.com/pod-product-compliance
Lightning Source LLC
Chambersburg PA
CBHW080610180526
45168CB00007B/2862